PENGUINS LIKE WARM CLIMATES TOO!

Animal Books for Kids 9-12
Children's Animal Books

Speedy Publishing LLC

40 E. Main St. #1156

Newark, DE 19711

www.speedypublishing.com

Copyright 2017

We think of penguins as living in Antarctica, at the bottom of the world, in a land of endless ice and snow. But there are many types of penguins that live far away from the South Pole. Read on and find out about them!

PENGUINS IN ALL SORTS OF PLACES

Penguins are cute and the whole world loves them. They rank with giant pandas as animals that people say, "Awww!" about. And they live in more places than we think they do.

Television shows tend to focus on Adelie and Emperor penguins in their huge rookeries in Antarctica, but those are just two species of penguins. Other species can be found in many other parts of the world.

But, just to be clear, there are no penguins at all at the North Pole!

ADELIE PENGUIN

GALAPAGOS PENGUIN

GALAPAGOS PENGUINS

Galapagos penguins live among the Galapagos Islands, about 600 miles west of South America and just above the equator. This makes them the only penguins you will ever see, outside of a zoo or an aquarium, in the Northern Hemisphere.

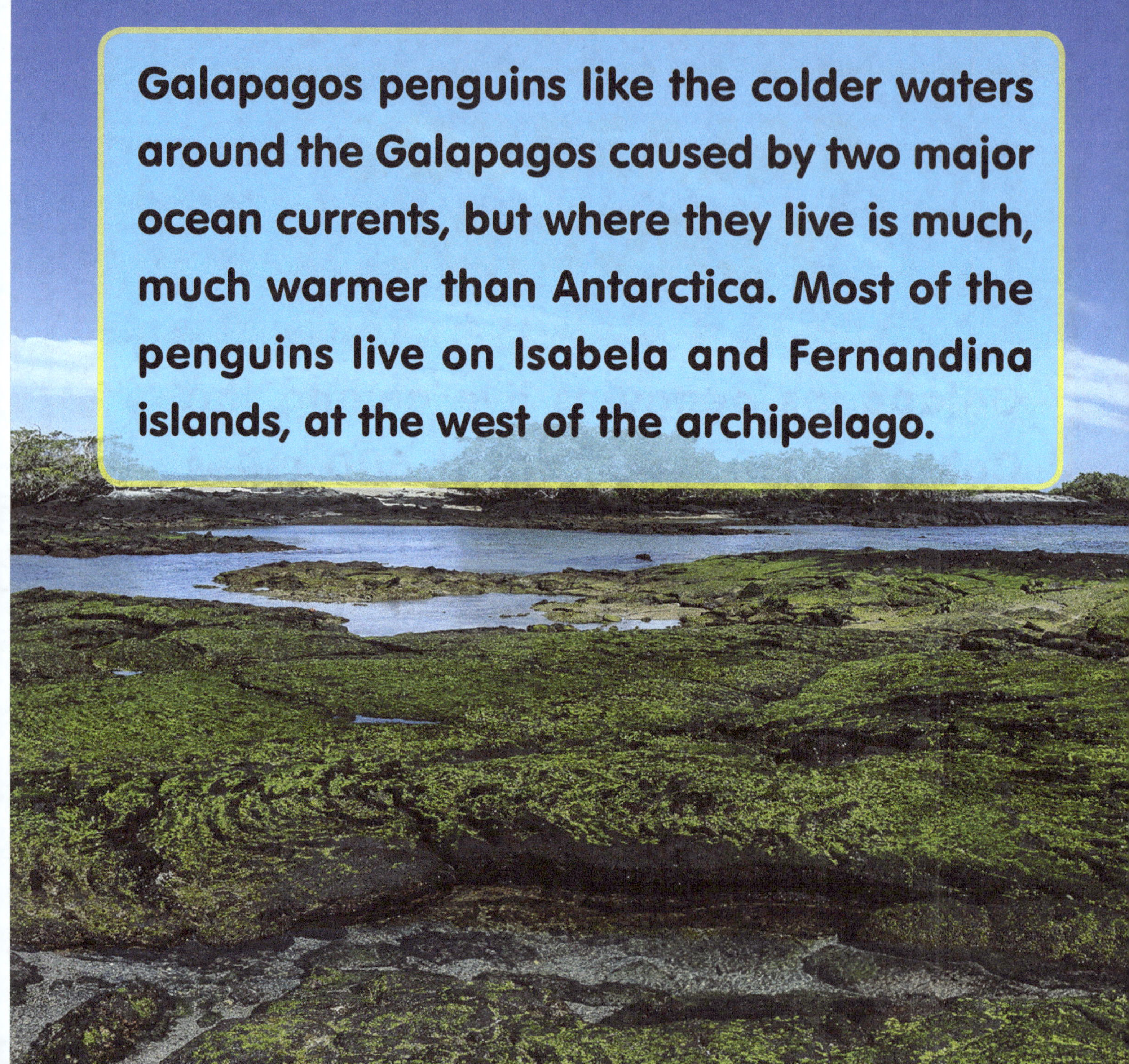

Galapagos penguins like the colder waters around the Galapagos caused by two major ocean currents, but where they live is much, much warmer than Antarctica. Most of the penguins live on Isabela and Fernandina islands, at the west of the archipelago.

FERNANDINA GALAPAGOS

To deal with the warmer climate, these penguins have ways of getting rid of excess heat. When they aren't in the water, they stretch their flippers wide and bend over to make a shadow over their feet so the sun does not warm them. They also pant like dogs.

The penguins lay their eggs in hidden places among the rocks on the islands to keep them from being overheated by the sun.

AFRICAN PENGUINS

African penguins are also called "jackass penguins" because they talk to each other using a loud braying sound, like a donkey. They live on the islands and coast of southern Africa.

AFRICAN PENGUIN

AFRICAN PENGUIN SWIMMING UNDERWATER

African penguins can stay under water for almost three minutes while they hunt anchovies, sardines, and squid to eat. They grow up to two feet tall and have short tails and wings that they use as flippers. They have thick, water-proof feathers that protect them against the cold water off the African coast.

Other penguins migrate to their breeding and nesting grounds, far from where they live other times of the year. African penguins don't travel to mate and have their babies.

They dig nests for their eggs and babies. They usually have two eggs at a time, and both parents help take care of them until they hatch. It takes up to four years for an African penguin to be old enough to have babies of its own.

FLOCK OF AFRICAN PENGUINS

Left alone, African penguins would live about 15 years. However, human activity keeps reducing their nesting sites, and over-fishing has made it harder for the penguins to find enough to eat. African penguins are now considered a highly-endangered species. Learn more about species at risk in the Baby Professor book **Vulnerable, Endangered, and Critically Endangered Animals**.

MAGELLANIC PENGUINS

Magellanic penguins live at the southern tip of South America, along the coasts of Argentina and Chile. They also breed on the Falkland Islands, off the Atlantic coast of Argentina. They are named to honor explorer Ferdinand Magellan, who reported seeing them in 1520.

MAGELLAN PENGUINS

KRILL

FLOCK OF MAGELLAN PENGUINS

FAMILY OF MAGELLAN PENGUINS

These penguins mate for life, raising a new baby each year. They can recognize each other just from hearing their calls.

PENGUINS OF NEW ZEALAND

There are two types of penguins on the coasts of New Zealand:

THE LITTLE PENGUIN

This species is also known as the blue or fairy penguin. It is the smallest penguin species. The chicks and young penguins have a clear blue color, which gives the species one of its names.

BLUE PENGUIN

BEAUTIFUL BEACH IN NEW ZEALAND

Little penguins live all around New Zealand and Tasmania, and along part of the southern coast of Australia. They are under threat from predators that humans introduced into the area, including cats and dogs.

THE YELLOW-EYED PENGUIN

The rarest penguin in the world, the yellow-eyed, lives along the coast of New Zealand. There are fewer than five thousand individuals left in the world. As you can imagine from their name, they have distinctive yellow eyes.

YELLOW-EYED PENGUIN

CASSOWARY

FUN PENGUIN FACTS

Here are some interesting things about penguins all the world over:

- Penguins are not the only birds who do not fly. They share the category of "flightless birds" with kiwis, ostriches, emus, and cassowaries, among other species. Most of these species live in the Southern Hemisphere.

- Young penguins in a group are called a crèche. A "raft" is the term for a group of penguins in the water, but on land a group of penguins is a "waddle"!

WATER POLLUTION

- There are about 17 penguin species in all, and 13 of them are considered endangered. Human activity and global warming, as well as the reduction of their food source, are putting all penguins under a threat of extinction. To learn more about the effects of global warming, read Baby Professor books like *What Every Child Should Know about Climate Change*.

- Penguins swallow small stones and use them to grind up their food so they can digest it more quickly. The extra weight may also help the penguins dive deeper in the water.

- Instead of teeth in their mouths, penguins have rows of spines on the inside of their upper beak and on their tongue to help them grip their food.

PENGUIN'S MOUTH

PENGUIN EATING FISH

- Penguins mostly eat fish and squid. A large penguin can swallow as many as thirty fish in a single dive!

- Those waterproof feathers need a lot of care, and penguins spend several hours a day grooming and putting their feathers in order. They have a special gland to produce oil that they put on their feathers to make them waterproof. Penguins have about 70 feathers per square inch, many more than most other birds.

- Once a year, penguins molt, losing all their feathers. Until their new feathers grow in, penguins can't go into the water and therefore can't hunt for food. The process can take weeks, and a penguin can lose as much as half of its weight before it is ready to hunt again.

MOLTING PENGUIN

KILLER WHALE

- Penguins like to travel, hunt, and bring up their babies together, in a group. A penguin colony can have millions of members. One reason they jump into the sea in large numbers together may be to confuse any waiting predators. There are so many tasty targets, the killer whale may miss getting any of them!

- Although penguins can swim as fast as 15 miles per hour in an emergency, they usually travel at about 5 mph through the water. On land, with that funny walk, they can only travel about two miles per hour!

- One reason that penguins can speed through the water when they need to is that they can cause a "bubble boost" by fluffing up their feathers to release air bubbles. The bubbles reduce the density of the water around the penguin and let them move more quickly.

PENGUINS SWIMMING AND JUMPING

- We have described the lands where penguins live outside of Antarctica, but most penguins spend three-quarters of their lives in the water. They are mainly creatures of the ocean, not of dry land.

- Although they act like fish, penguins don't have gills and can't breathe water. They can stay under water for a very long time, but then they have to come to the surface to get more air, just like whales or dolphins.

- **Scientists think that penguins may be very nearsighted when they are on land. Their eyes are designed to work better under water.**

- **Prehistoric penguins could be very large. Some of them were almost six feet tall!**

PENGUIN SKELETON

- **The oldest known penguin fossil is from almost sixty million years ago, and was found in Antarctica.**

- **When penguins are swimming fast, they use a technique called "porpoising". They leap as high as seven feet out of the water, grabbing the air they need while still moving forward.**

- Isabelline penguins is a term for baby penguins of many species that are born with brown feathers instead of black ones. They tend to live shorter lives because their camouflage is not as good as that of their brothers and sisters with black feathers. About one in fifty thousand babies has brown feathers.

PENGUIN WITH GENETIC DISORDER

IN THE AIR AND THE SEA, AND ON DRY LAND

Animals of all kinds share this world with us. Learn about more of them in Baby Professor books like Just Keep Swimming!, The World's Most Beautiful Birds, and Dogs and Cats.

Visit

BABY PROFESSOR
EDUCATION KIDS

www.BabyProfessorBooks.com
to download Free Baby Professor eBooks and view
our catalog of new and exciting Children's Books